Glory River

 Southern Messenger Poets

DAVE SMITH, Series Editor

~~~~~~~~~ *Glory River* ~~~~~~~~~

poems

DAVID HUDDLE

LOUISIANA STATE UNIVERSITY PRESS)|(*Baton Rouge*

For John Engles, 1921–2007

Published by Louisiana State University Press
Copyright © 2008 by David Huddle
All rights reserved
Manufactured in the United States of America
FIRST PRINTING

Designer: AMANDA MCDONALD SCALLAN
Typeface: BASKERVILLE
Printer and binder: THOMSON-SHORE, INC.

Library of Congress Cataloging-in-Publication Data

Huddle, David, 1942–
 Glory river : poems / David Huddle.
  p. cm. — (Southern messenger poets)
 ISBN 978-0-8071-3306-4 (cloth : alk. paper) — ISBN 978-0-8071-3307-1 (pbk. : alk. paper)
 I. Title.
 PS3558.U287G57 2007
 811'.54—dc22

The author wishes to thank the editors of the following journals, in which some of these poems were previously published: *ABZ, Appalachian Heritage, Blackbird, Florida Review, Georgia Review, Hampden-Sydney Poetry Review, Shenandoah, Southern Review,* and *Yale Review.*

Contents

~ I ~
River

Courting

When a man loves a woman in Glory
River, she runs like fire if she knows what's
good for her—& most don't, we admit that much—
because any boy grows up here gets Ugly

for his middle name. Our boys don't know how
to take a girl to Hester's Drive-In & hold
her hand or call her up & tell her she's
pretty or just plant a soft little kiss

right below her earlobe—that's not the way
we do it. We take her for a ride & jack
the truck up to a hundred, scare a cold sweat
out of her, then run a hand up her skirt

& get slapped good. Timing's got to be exact.
Look at that moon, we say in dulcet tones,
jerking a thumb—*Got my guitar in the back.*
Thought maybe you'd like to hear some George Jones.

The Mouth of Him

Rule of thumb—whatever came out of that mouth
was not what you wanted
to hear—*Underarm hair! Belly lint! Your mother's*
a giraffe, your daddy plays
string mop in the swamps of Arkansas. More smarts
in my buttocks,
more truth between my toes, though truth was not a lot
of words came out
of that mouth, even though words damn sure came
to mind if you cast
your eyes in the direction of his face. Thin-lipped,
a crooked slash,
a straight line at an angle, that mouth often as not
dangled a cigarette,
or spat a nasty stream of old grasshopper juice, yeah,
that's right, that mouth
wasn't designed to charm you debutante delicates. Man's
blue-jawed & pale-skinned
as a Goodyear whitewall & the jaw itself has a hard
twitch like he's about
to clock you one, but then he turns & presses a thumb
to his nose & snorts out
a snot plug & turns back & maybe even steps up face
to face with you—*Ricochet*
rugrat & switchback, he says, *all the way to Toledo,*
bungholes & rosehips
like you know what he means, which you do more or less, or
you could translate it
into a story he doesn't tell with that lizard sultry Dick
Tracy Valentino ugly
mouth of his—There was this woman went with him to a bar
& she wasn't troubled
that he wouldn't say anything, or when he did, it wasn't

words fit for human ears,
she liked it well enough just that way & so she fixes her
eyes on that mouth
of his & when he starts to whisper *Ignominy bowling ball
hyena & hippo*—she shushes
the man, puts a finger to his lips, dares touch the holy
place. "Shut up!"
rasps she & shocks him out of saying *Bailiwick porcupine
rutabaga blue balls* as he wants
to mutter; he just up & shuts up & she fixes her eyes again
on the mouth of him
& her own mouth falls agape & after awhile a shaking
transmogrifies her whole
body & that shocks him, & so he starts up another of his
beyond the grave utterances—
Hippodrome onomatopoeia nation states midnight conundrum,
he says, that mouth
inexpressive as a mudcat on the river bottom but moving
nevertheless—*Fickle
altimeter shotgun,* he says, & *wherein are gathered worms
worse than facts,*
but now she listens & smiles & stands up & takes the man
in her arms not
for a kiss or what you might call a hug but like you might
apply some kind
of medical apparatus, she pulls him to her—almost *into*
her—if you can feature
such an embrace, so that he can't get his breath but she's
pig-iron strong
& then she really shivers like she's in the death throes
till she picks him up
& finally casts him aside, flings him like blanket thrown
off on a hot night
& he falls on the floor of the barroom & looks up at her—

What the hell?
he starts, but she stares him down—*Mushroom beleaguered*
pantaloon! she shouts,
barely moving her steely lips. *Coliseums of beasties &*
paratrooping oscilloscopes
grunge gouge & galumph by the surge of these silly waters.
Festoon thyself
Festoon thyself! she advises him & walks out—which was
of course the end
of him as we knew him there along the barren banks of the
Glory River
in those long ago days when we'd fallen silent & paralyzed
under the dictatorship
of his mothering mouth that now says *Pass the salt please*
& *May I be excused?*

The Last Time Anything Went

Muddy days descended into the valley
there by Glory River, cold fronts sweeping
all the way down from Saskatchewan to freeze
up our desire for sex & old movies, &
I have to tell you, too, Anything fucked
everything in sight—raccoons, cows, tin cans,
even thistles sometimes when he wanted
to prove a point—but I loved that stinker,
I loved him bad & would have sucked his dick
in Winchester Cathedral on Easter Sunday,
though of course I couldn't tell him that.
The thing about Anything was whatever
or whomever you loved, he'd go off & just
casually diddle it so you couldn't care
about it anymore, & if he knew you'd gone
sweet on him, why then he'd figure out a way
to strobe-blink your eyesight, stick a stink-pod
up your nose, at night he'd sneak up & lay
a cocklebur under your tongue, then make
your ears start screaming like Jerry Lee
Lewis, he'd make your fingertips feel
hammerblows every time you thought about
running a sweet touch down his pretty chest.
So it wasn't grand being around a mother-
humper like that—if you got a little jolt
of happiness, rest assured Anything would be
dumping coyote turds all over you before
you could even figure out the source
of your joy. Then after he went—& you know
how he does it, just ups & twitches a face at you
& out the door—we all lay around the river-
bank, leafing through old Sears catalogs

& picking our scabs, & nobody saying doodly
squat but everybody hoping he'd come
bopping back down the slag-heap, yodeling like
Caruso being put to death, & start
making our lives miserable again. That's when
Ellen over there invented the Anything Prayer.
One morning she just stood up & stretched—
& my God, does that woman have a set
of boobies that say hello when she lifts
her arms to the sky. *Listen to this,* she says,
I do hereby implore the mighty powers
that give out Cadillac SUVs, starve babies
in Ethiopia, bomb civilians in Iraq,
& generally & randomly humiliate,
exfoliate, & exterminate. I do hereby
humbly request the return of Anything.
As I stand here with my perfectly human
arms raised to the whimsy of outer space,
I beseech the irascible hegemony
up there behind that Carolina blue
to give us back our own personal bliss-killing
party-pooping life-shredder, the only one
who truly knows how to turn our days
into toxic dog biscuits. Almighty Whatever,
lest we perish here by the Glory
River in our squalor & sloth, our lethargy
& our interior desert, please just give us
back our beloved sublimely nasty &
transformational butt-fucker Anything.

Metamorphosis

Was a girl in Glory River—
    plain girl, nothing to her, really, girl
        of small note while she was growing up
            except she was maybe more tomboy than most

till her tenth year when this little
    something happened—she was playing
        in the town branch, with Gilmer Hyatt
            & Tommy Ingo & Trenton Mabe, with Willa Pope

kind of hanging back cause
    she didn't want to get her drawers
        wet in that muddy old branch water
            & this child—whose name was Sarah Jean

& who was the best crawdad
    hunter of that generation of our valley's
        branch splashers & minnow-seiners & other
            such muddy urchins as had scuttered up

& down that little spring-fed driblet
    of a stream throughout our dissolute history,
        fathers & mothers having done it, as far
            back as anybody could recall, but Sare—

as Gilmer & that gang called her—
    caught crawdads like she was half
        crawdad herself, but it was because
            she wasn't afraid of the pincers,

plus she didn't care if she caught
    them, she just liked the cold water
        tickling her ankles & shins, liked
            the smell of mint & watercress when

you shoved the seine into it
    & loved the shine of the minnows
        in the sunlight when you brought up
            the seine & they flopped across the net

& so on this midsummer afternoon
    these children were in the spell
        of the sunlight & heat & grasshoppers
            & cicada hum & june bugs & honeysuckle

& they had their bucket for what
    water creatures they caught & they
        were quiet as if at work on some
            school project with a teacher

hovering over their shoulders
    except it was just the summer spell
        when time stops for a child & lets
            her float into some other macrocosm

where school & parents
    & books & yelling & hitting
        & being afraid—all of that isn't
            there, it's only the murmuring

stream, heat on your shoulders, a cold
    swirl around your feet, when of a sudden
        Sarah Jean—pants rolled up & splashed
            & her brother's old shirt wet, too—

Sarah Jean stood up straight
    in the middle of the branch
        & held up her palm, water
            glistening down her arm

& she was just so charmed
　　with what she had, a tadpole
　　　　squirming across the shiny map
　　　　　　of her cupped hand, brown jewel

that her eyes adored so much
　　she whispered to it & the other
　　　　children seeing her face so radiant
　　　　　　stood & gathered around her, as if

they hadn't seen ten thousand
　　tadpoles before, but now this one
　　　　Sarah Jean had lifted into the light
　　　　　　enthralled them & so it was correct

for Sarah Jean to close
　　her other hand over the wriggling
　　　　little thing, it was as if they
　　　　　　wanted her to do just that & she did

& brought both hands down
　　to her chest & held them there
　　　　cupped together & some later said
　　　　　　Sare even closed her eyes & moved

her lips, though Sarah Jean herself
　　said no, it wasn't like that, she just
　　　　stood still because she felt something
　　　　　　like a wind moving through her, & so

when her hands came open
　　& it was a green frog there
　　　　for just the moment before
　　　　　　it sprang from her hands

into the water & darted
   into the green weeds & was gone
      she felt as if she'd been asleep
        & now was suddenly awake back

into the world she knew, Glory
   River Valley & this little creek
      & this day & her friends staring
        at her & all she could do was laugh

which made everything
   snap back into place
      except Gilmer & Tommy
        whooped & took the seine

& plunged it into the weeds
   where the green frog had darted
      & they all made a grand commotion
        trying to find the frog, which might

never have been anything
   but a dream anyway, all of them
      ready to swear they'd seen it,
        frog like no other thing they'd seen

in all their years, though no such
   frog appeared to them again that day
      or any other & Sarah Jean, a.k.a. Sare—
        not because of anything she did or said—

became the one they couldn't leave
   alone, though they couldn't decide
      what to make of her, how to treat her,
        or what to do when they were around her,

some tripped her or shoved her
or hit her in the back & ran
but some brought her presents & sat
by her & shared their brown bag

lunches with her & Tommy Ingo
swore he loved her & would marry her
when they got old enough, but then
he got stomped to death by his grandad's

cantankerous old bull
& on into her early teens
girls sought Sare out one day
as their friend & next day

declared they hated her
& boys approached & tried
to look her in the eye & say
something smart or nasty

& when she started riding
the bus to high school
kids would touch her
on the shoulder, her arm

or hand, her hair, & all
the while our Sarah Jean lived
her life like any girl would
& she wasn't pretty or even

all that smart, wasn't shy
but mostly kept quiet, it made
no difference, the kids made fools
of themselves around her & couldn't

hurt her enough to change her
    & couldn't flatter her enough
        to turn her into a prisspot
            but then when she was old

enough that her parents let her
    go out with boys in cars, boys fought
        over her & girls started hating her
            more than ever & then Trenton, who'd

been her quiet & unacknowledged
    servant since the day of the green frog,
        hit a Wytheville boy in the face & broke
            his teeth so the parents brought charges

& Trenton got sent to jail
    & never was the same again
        & a boy named Orvil Harrison
            from Cripple Creek took our Sare

to the drive-in a couple of times
    & some said they saw those two kissing
        & twisting around in the car instead
            of watching the movies & so it was no

surprise that two cars
    ran Orvil off the highway
        late one night after he'd taken
            our Sarah Jean home & the wreck

broke Orvil's back
    & he was in a wheelchair ever after
        & after that Sarah Jean said she'd never
            go out with any boy ever again & she

swore she'd stay home
    & try to look after her mom
        who'd become both feeble & loony
            in her worrying over Sarah Jean

& of course her father
    had run off with Willa Pope
        & they'd relocated over to Tazewell
            & the old man never sent money & blamed

Sarah Jean for making him
    unhappy at home & so Sare
        & her mother had to sell the house
            for almost nothing & buy a trailer

up on Rakestown Ridge where
    the dirt road comes into Route 93
        & still even though she was almost
            invisible up there, just walked

down to Collins's Shell Station
    to get what groceries she & her mother
        had to have, & even though her clothes
            were nothing you or I would ever wear,

somehow we couldn't forget
    & people wouldn't leave her
        alone, people threw things
            at her out their car windows

if they saw her walking
    & Glen Riggins claimed he spat
        on her one time & then old Leena Grimes
            hanging up a wash out beside her house

saw Sare come walking up
     the road & something got
          into Leena & she knelt down
               right there underneath the clothesline

& stayed on her knees
     until our Sarah Jean was out
          of sight & even though Sare
               probably never even noticed

what Leena had done, Leena
     told about it, said she didn't
          know why she did it & she wished
               somebody would tell her why she'd done it

but people didn't like
     Leena's story, Kent Fulcher
          told her to keep her mouth shut
               about that kind of thing & it

wasn't more than a week
     after that that the trailer
          where Sarah Jean & her mother
               lived went up in flames—this

was after midnight & they
     must have been sound asleep
          & nobody was out to see what
               happened, but they said it was

like a bomb had hit it,
     like an air force jet
          had swept down & dropped
               napalm on that trailer

& they say the flames
   shot three hundred yards up
      into the sky & it burnt like
         dry forest wood, burnt so hot

there was nothing left
   for the fire department
      to save when they got there
         & so they just watched it

& the next morning every bit
   of that trailer was gone,
      just a pit of ashes & smoke,
         nothing left, no evidence a person

like Sarah Jean
   had ever lived
      here in Glory River
         or anywhere else.

Screech Owl

This scientist came to Glory River
to tell us we should be proud of our owl
population. Nobody laughed out loud—
you'd have thought we were like Wytheville
or at least Max Meadows people we made
such proper manners.
                              No scientist could
know Bill Stoots would as soon spit Red Man
in his face, or George Carey would trip him
to watch him fall or that Thelma Roberts grabs
a man's crotch if she feels like it, just to see
what he'll do—he was ignorant of us
& what we did to that Massachusetts
woman who came through here with her little tape
recorder three years ago.
                              Brother Screech Owl
we came to call him in the week he spent
with us, camped out in his tidy blue tent
down by the river not so far from where
the card players carry on all night—
                              that's why
Bill Pike took it upon himself to wake
the man up well after midnight & ask
him what importance a Screech Owl was & why
had he come nosing around in our valley
to look at something most people never saw
or cared about anyway? if there were
Screech Owls in Glory River, well so what?—
didn't they belong to us & didn't
he know we didn't like strangers minding
Glory River's business, or coming in here
for any reason whatsoever, not to mention
looking at our critters & varmints?

crawled out of his tent, rubbing his eyes
& we saw he couldn't see much without
his glasses, but he seemed to realize
he was being called out to speak to us
& if he didn't find the right words
he & his tent both might be taking a swim
in the dark.

      My friends, he said & we got
quiet because as he spoke he started
lifting his arms out like airplane wings.
My friends, an owl could be flying this way
right this moment, and we would never hear
the creature because it has tiny fringe-
like structures along the outer edge
of each feather. The salamander two feet
from your own foot could be snatched up into
its talons without you ever hearing a sound.
My friends, he said, *by day the Screech Owl sits*
quietly among the branches of a tree.
If danger threatens, the little owl
protects itself by elongating its body
and extending its ear tufts to resemble
and blend into the tree branches. It shuts
its eyes down to a mere slit and it sits
perfectly still until the threat has passed.
You have to understand, my friends, he said,
a screech owl is not much bigger than your fist
—and he balled up his to show us—*but it's*
just so smart, and it's a fierce hunter.

Then the scientist put his arms down
at his sides & just stood there in front
of his pitiful little tent like he knew

he'd had his say, & he was right about that.
What we knew that he didn't was his life
was in the hands of Bill Pike, foremost
drunk of Glory River Valley & illegitimate
son of a great family of drunks
                         & Bill Pike
turned around to the little crowd of us
standing there behind him & we could see
his banged up face & seldom combed hair & his one
half cut-off ear & Bill was crazy angry,
we could see that, which made a murmur rise
up from among us, because used as we are to
fighting & killing, not a one of us wanted
to see that scientist die right then—
                         which was
exactly the moment when Deetum Dunford,
Monkey's boy that never had been right, you could
see from his angel face, a man that picked berries
all summer for money & lived in little camps
he made all up & down the river & fished even
through the winter—that was when Deetum
walked up from behind us & we hadn't heard him
or known he was anywhere near—that was when
Deetum walked up through the little crowd
of us, with this feathered thing perched on his arm,
& it seemed to be sleeping while Deetum
carried it along—we could tell he was trying
to walk soft & even so as not to disturb it,
brownish thing with sort of gray streaks, & we
got just so still & quiet that it nearly made us
shit our pants when it opened these huge eyes
& rotated its head all around like it meant
to see every last one of us & take note of us

with its lantern eyes & my God, did we stare
at it & it at us, Bill Pike shrinking back
a step when Deetum stepped up beside him.
                                        Deetum
reached the thing to the scientist, & they
had to work with the laces Deetum had tied
around its feet to get it from the one arm
to the other, & the owl let it happen, all
the while just staring out at us, swiveling
that head around,
                        & Bill Pike faded back through
the crowd of us
                        & the scientist said,
"Thank you, Mr. Dunford, how much do I owe you?"
& Deetum shook his head, so shy was he that he
hardly ever took money from anybody,
& the scientist said, "I thank you, sir."

& that was the end of it—next morning
the blue tent was not there, the jeep was gone,
the scientist was never seen again here
in our valley, & Bill Pike was never the same
again either, got to be a sweet drunk
instead of the mean one he'd been all those
years, which was a notable improvement,
because he'd been a bad influence on us
all his grown-up life.
                        Everybody said it was
the Screech Owl cure that fixed him up, which is
of course the kind of thing we like to say
here in Glory River—it gives us pleasure.

The Cosmetic Surgeon Comes to Glory River

Comes he, of the steely case of instruments,
   of the happy juice that sends us to cuddle with God,
      of the slimy manner that persuades us to nod & affix

our fatuous signatures to his papers,
   that has us fingering up whatever moneys
      made their way into our pockets, however we got it

nobody's business, but now our crumpled bills flying
   over to him of the white tunic & the sharpest edges
      anyone along these muddy banks had ever touched—

it was the knives that inveigled us,
   such pleasant little things, & he said
      they would make us more resplendent in our parts,

which, too, stimulated our imaginations—
   that we could become comely in our privates,
      because here along the river we had only Patricia

whom we worshipped for her milky skin
   & righteous cleavage but most especially
      for the splendor of her vaginal territory—

so esteemed was this anatomical wonder
   that Patricia allowed us a yearly viewing,
      the crowd of us mud-bespattered citizens

stretching nearly back to Fort Besotted
   because everyone wanted to see, no one wished
      to miss his or her annual glimpse of Patricia

smiling & standing in the sunlit shallows
   of the Glory River, her pastel skirts raised
      & gathered at her waist & nary an undergarment

to hinder anyone's vision of her argillaceous skin,
    the flaxen curls tufted sweetly there at the crux
        of her thighs just inches above the chilly flow

of our own brown swirling waters
    & you may ask why we lived as we did
        there in our polluted & trash-ridden valley

seeking solace in such barbarous rituals
    as the viewing of our Patricia's centerpiece,
        as it were, & the answer is at least as natural

as bootleg by the fire or tossing our cans out
    into the rapids to watch them bob & float & sink—
        our lives were small & hateful as the withered hibiscus

of our childhoods, & so our silly dream of coupling
    —or maybe just a little lusty affection—with Patricia,
        persuading that dear girl that it was you she had sought

all this time, you who must be invited into her interior,
    so to speak—well, every man, woman, & child of our soiled
        community entertained these idiotic fantasies because sex

for us was shattered & dissolved & obfuscated
    so that we were passionate but unclear about our lusts
        & desires—we wanted, oh yes we wanted each other & animals

& objects, our wants boldly asserted themselves
    & we became tolerant of them in each other & sometimes
        submitted or enabled or merely watched an awful unlikely

coupling of some sort, but not one of us
    was consistent—so fickle were we that what
        we wanted yesterday we spurned today or sometimes

we even changed mid-act & left the diddling
    of one sex to take up with another & registered
        such love-treachery with only the merest shrug

& our confusion made us objects of scorn & derision
    elsewhere & everywhere but here, there were even flirtation
        laws against us in Wytheville & Roanoke, laws forbidding

us to travel beyond our nasty valley, laws monsterizing
    us throughout America, & yet throughout our oppression,
        there was Patricia & the seasonal viewing of her pudendum

that gave us pride & steadied us—that is, until came he
    of the case of blue steel instruments, the little sharpies
        & the promise of upgrading our parts, maybe even making

us candidates for Patricia's favors, & so stepped forth
    our Jack Haskins, a.k.a. Jack the Insignificant, for alas,
        living as we lived, rarely copulating out of sight & often

attracting an audience—what else did we have
    for entertainment?—for our carnal acts were public,
        our anatomies known generally & frequently discussed

& so poor Jack Haskins was often mocked to his face
    for the modesty of his endowment, & we thought it
        meet & right for our Jack to seek improvement, call it

cosmetic or whatever, & so he steps forward
    & shows the cutter his stash of greenbacks,
        & those two canter away to the huckleberry

grove, where as it happens, the field version
    of a surgery has been set up, a masked nurse,
        gloved hands lifted, awaits surgeon & surgeree

& they duck into the tent, which denies us vision
  of the procedure & we mill around outside, grumbling
    our complaints, & now & then shouting & demanding

that the tent flaps be lifted & the democracy
  of seeing everything be reestablished, for that is
    how it had always been in our valley, however loathsome

or disgraceful a human transaction might be
  we carried it out openly & sometimes criticized
    or happily labeled it unethical or mean or petty

but no matter, things went on in full sight
  of our citizenry, & so the visual privatizing
    of this new & revolutionary event of genitalia

modification angered us or at least made us surly
  & restless there in the huckleberry grove, some
    tossed bottles against rocks, some tossed old cans

against the tent sides, & a chant had started
  to arise amongst us—*Let Us See! Let Us See!*—
    when suddenly out steps Jack in his old shirt

but naked below the waist, & by God yes he was
  letting us see & what we saw shut us up good,
    our Jack Haskins had become Jack the Notable

for verily I tell you, what had been of #2 pencil
  girth had now become planklike & astonishingly
    admirable in its eager demeanor, & our formerly

modest Jack now displayed himself, turned this way
  & that & a murmuring broke out among us, then some
    applauding & cheers, & before Jack finished bowing

& pantsed himself, our Esther Hamilton scuttered
   out of the crowd of us & ducked into the tent, not
      even asking or bargaining, just shot herself into

the place where Jack's miracle had occurred, & no one
   objected because our abject Esther, though she'd kept
      herself covered for all of her adult life, was known

to possess labia of comical size & configuration,
   oh a sad circumstance to be cursed in such a way—
      even in our valley where dignity was too scarce

to be an issue in every case except that of our Patricia—
   our Esther had had not a single sexual encounter that any
      among us had witnessed & so was our sad case, our Lady

of the Misshapen Labia, & so to honor her we kept
   silent as we stood or squatted or hunkered down
      outside the tent & we hoped for rectification

for Esther, & we had more or less forgotten
   about the stranger with the knives, the specialist
      who'd come to our valley, he of the instruments

remained out of sight, & our Esther was in the tent
   for such a long while that we grew fearful & sad
      & thought poor Esther might have died on the table,

for after all, wasn't this a crude thing
   that had been set up, as for a battlefield?
      & twilight began to settle down upon us, the light

deepening in that way that suggests death
   & a murmur came up among us, but just then
      our Esther steps shyly out onto the muddy place

in front of the tent & with the nurse shining
    a flashlight upon her, our Esther lifts her skirt
        & there before our eyes is as elegant a vaginal

configuration as ever has been witnessed
    or even dreamed of by any of us, surpassing
        even the charm of our Patricia, & our Patricia

lets out a shriek of rage & despair & faints
    down into the mud, for she realizes she has
        been displaced, has been diminished down into

merely one of us & some of us go to comfort her
    because the belittling of a beloved one is never
        what we like, even we lowly residents of Glory

River hate it when what is grand suddenly
    becomes common, which is generally the way of it
        here, & then a line forms at the tent & surgical

procedures proceed throughout the evening
    & the deep night & on into the rosy morning,
        our citizenry entering the tent & exiting

with our improvements, showing off ourselves
    for all to see, for with the refurbishment
        of our parts, we became proud & piss-ant vain,

& when it was done, when the instruments
    had had their way with us & he who diddled
        the knives into our flesh & enhanced & modified

& magnified or subtracted, when he had extracted
    all such cash moneys as could be had from our valley,
        why then he struck the tent & with his still masked

& gloved nurse rode away from Glory River
    his sleek SUV sprouting great plumes of mud
        as he sped toward the greater world of Wytheville

& Roanoke & perhaps even Charlottesville,
    & some remembered how the instruments clattered
        in their case, or how some seepage that might

have been our very own blood seemed to drip
    from the vehicle as it left & some said he flung
        little bits & pieces of us out his vehicle's windows

as it fled our valley, but these rumors were
    quick to fade because by then we had become
        so godlike & obnoxious we hardly took interest

in each other at all anymore & some of us
    went out into the greater world & flirted
        & seduced & fornicated as the ordinary

ones had always done & children were conceived
    & born & eventually Glory River itself suffered
        a betterization, our trash was picked up, our cans

& bottles recycled, our muddy paths graveled
    into nature trails, even the turd-pocked waters
        of the stream itself were treated & cleansed & yet

there remains in a secluded cove downstream
    where no one ever goes anymore, a marble statue
        of our Patricia out in the shallows, her skirt

raised & gathered about her waist, her face
    turned up to smile at those invisible ones
        who come to pay homage to how it used to be.

Pity

Save your prayers—we Glory River rats
don't need you putting in a good word
for us. God damn right, love is fucking mess
here in the valley. Theater of the Absurd

acted out daily down at the post office
& Miss Janie's Beauty Parlor, wives dumped
beside the road, husbands shot or knifed twice—
front & back—kids emotionally stomped,

parents out looking for more of the same.
You think you've got it better, don't you? Well,
God loves us, too! Above average pain
makes us what you might call unpredictable

& mean, but what we've got that you don't is
this fiddle, banjo, & stand-up bass, this
steel guitar—Do you hear that? Blood & dirt,
love come & gone in a truckload of hurt.

The Mayor of Glory River

Was a dog that made them laugh—named Copacetic,
Muhammad, Sam, Federal Government,
Nicodemus, Doctor Pepper, Blackie,
Mayor Dog, Mississippi, Winston
Churchill, whatever name came to mind
when the dog was around: It came to me
to use this joke in my dissertation—
the legendary many-named cur
embodying a contemptuous attitude
toward authority tacitly
shared by residents of Glory River,
a convergence of Appalachian humor,
dialect, and the shared values peculiar
to their microregion. The impulse to name
and to improvise laconically
seemed to me so purely Anglo-American
that when the idea struck, I imagined—
as clearly as if I'd already written them—
fifty brilliant pages published
as the lead essay in the Journal
of Appalachian Studies.
                                    I want to
show you something about this dog, Joe Lee
Liggins told me during my interview
with him outside Collins's Shell Station
one afternoon. Joe Lee stood, put his hands
in his pockets and as he whistled a soft
ditty while smiling slyly at me, aimed
a quick, hard kick at the Mayor's head. The dog
had been lying at our feet, as if to listen
to our conversation, but he seemed not
at all surprised—as I most certainly was—

by the sudden assault of Joe Lee's foot. At
the exact moment necessary not
to be where the boot would have struck, he stood.
Rising to his four feet, the Mayor seemed calm
and not at all insulted. He stretched in that
canine way, a bow that appears to mock
whoever witnesses it—
                    which bow led
Joe Lee to pivot and direct another kick
at the Mayor's tail-becrested butt, but
the dog sat, again casually but at just
the moment to evade the kick by the width
of one of his whiskers. Then the Mayor
scratched and licked himself, as if his safety
were not an issue.
                    Do you see what I mean?
Joe Lee asked me.
                    I knew what I'd seen, yet
I doubted it. I'm not superstitious,
and so to me the dog's evasions were
remarkable coincidences that appeared
miraculous but weren't. The dog's yawning
and curling up again at our feet as Joe Lee
took his seat on a Pepsi crate made him seem
all the more ordinary. The Mayor was wiry
and coal black except for white on his chest,
a sort of greyhound-great-Dane-Labrador,
a large enough animal that his back
was about the height of my hip bone
when I stood but delicate as a deer
or panther—and evidently sweet-natured.
True, he had amber eyes in his blocklike
head and these gave him a hound-from-hell look,

but his general demeanor was cheerful,
friendly, solicitous, which is to say
that even with what I'd witnessed, I'd have sworn
he was your normal dog, basic as weather,
weeds, or oatmeal.
                              Should I fetch the shotgun
and show you the same thing again? Joe Lee asked,
but I waved my hand and said no, no, I
understood the lesson he'd taught me. This must
have been what Joe Lee wanted me to say—
he smiled, nodded, sat down, took a dip of snuff,
leaned back on his crate, crossed his arms, and waited
for me to continue interviewing him.
And I must say that the people I met
in Glory River spoke freely and at some
length, as if they wanted to explain how
in that place they had become the people
they were. Murders, unusually random violence,
incest, thefts, car wrecks, hatred, rage,
strange loyalties, anarchy, paranoia,
irrational fears, prejudice—it all had a kind
of meaning to them, a logic that became
more and more evident to me the longer
I stayed among them, the more I listened
to the stories they told. I sometimes thought
I'd begun to see the world as they saw
it, and so I'd be doomed to live in that
valley, where a dog was the resident
magician, witch doctor, and messiah,
where the fiery death of Sarah Jean Kinney
and her mother was mostly what everybody
wanted to talk about, and where if you lived
there long enough you grew to be unfit

to live anywhere else.
                              Joe Lee Liggins
was a classic citizen—Pepsi crate pundit,
a veritable campaign manager,
happy to glorify the Mayor all day,
if I wanted to listen and take notes while
the Mayor himself licked his genitalia.
Joe Lee claimed that Deetum Dunford was the first
to meet the Mayor, and for some months people
thought the dog belonged to Deetum, who called
him Catfish. Deetum said he'd been fishing
with no luck throughout a long afternoon,
was about to give it up and go home
and fix himself a mayonnaise sandwich,
when of a sudden Catfish just kind of
appeared beside him, lying down right there
in the grass and observing Deetum's line
and bobber out in the water. Before Deetum
had time to wonder where the dog had come from,
he started catching smallmouth bass, one
after another, as fast as he could reel them in,
bait his hook, and throw the line out again.
There on the riverbank, it was that last
swatch of daylight just before it's too dark
for a fisherman to see what he's doing,
but Deetum says he caught his whole stringer
full of bass in maybe fifteen minutes.
Then the dog followed him home—or what Deetum
called home, which is what you and I would call
camp. Worried about having too many fish
to eat, Deetum couldn't stand to let good
food go to waste, but he needn't have worried
because the dog was happy to gnash down

those lard-fried filets, too. They finished off
all the fish that evening.

Deetum thought he had
himself a dog, a real fine fishing dog,
but the Mayor was gone the next morning,
and Deetum didn't see him again until
two days later, by himself as usual,
fishing at the same spot and catching
nothing whatsoever until there
the dog was again, lying in the grass beside
him, studying the line and bobber out
in the water. Then just like that, the fish
started biting so fast and hard it was
like they wanted to jump out of the water
and into Deetum's lap.

Leena Grimes was
the next one to get a visit from the dog,
and she called him Midnight because that's
about when he appeared on her front porch.
It was July, a hot spell when everybody
had trouble sleeping, but Leena never much
minded weather like that, she enjoyed
sitting on her porch glider deep into
the early hours of the morning, just gently
touching a toe down every once in a while
to make the thing sway back and forth, half
asleep and feeling like she had one foot
in a dream, the other right there in Glory
River. Then she noticed what she first thought
a shadow but was in fact a black dog lying
on the porch close enough to bite her ankle
if he'd wanted to. Though she'd never seen
him before, she said he had the feel and manner

of a dog that might have belonged to her
for a long time—so she just spoke to him
that way. *Hello, Midnight,* she said she said.
The animal lifted its head and stared
at her as if to say, *What do you want?*
During my interview with Leena, she
admitted that she'd always loved magic,
and so she didn't trust herself in thinking
that finally she'd gotten her deepest
wish, a dog that could change her bad luck.
Because Leena's story was one of the saddest
I heard in all my time in Glory River,
a husband who'd been killed by a drunk driver,
a son who was in jail for bootlegging—
a bootlegger stupid enough to get caught—
and a daughter who walked the streets—those were
Leena's words, *walked the streets*—of Baltimore.

That was the morning the dog got his title.
In his high-stepping, royal dog manner,
he walked beside Leena to the post office,
where Robert Alley, sitting on the steps
out there, touched the brim of his Blue Seal cap
and said, *Good morning, Leena, I see you're
walking with the Mayor this morning.* Leena
said she both knew and didn't know what Robert
was talking about, but it amused her, so that
she was giggling when she went in to ask
for her mail. That was when Elwood told her there
was a letter she'd have to sign for before
he could give it to her.
                              Leena never told what
came to her in that envelope—like most

Glory River people, she was perfectly
open about not revealing the crucial
details of some stories. All she would say was
They found land on my property, and the phrase
pleased her mightily when she said it.

You'd have
thought Leena would have moved out of the valley—
evidently she came into a lot of money,
because she fixed up her house higgeldy-
piggeldy, as is the way among those people,
had indoor plumbing installed, added a room here,
a room there, and painted it the gaudiest
shade of lavender she could find. She said
she wouldn't dream of leaving Glory River,
it was a rough place to live, and she knew
it wasn't going to change, but it was home
for her. She commissioned Dude Dunford
to construct a palatial dog house
in the side yard, and when it was finished,
she went to considerable trouble to persuade
the Mayor to live in it. The dog sometimes
dropped by for one of Leena's snacks, and she said
that in the course of time he'd peed on all four
corners of his mansion but that he'd made it
clear to her that the place didn't suit him.
She confessed that the Mayor never sat
with her on the porch again.

Baron Gomes was
who he took up with next, a white boy thought
to have been fathered by Buddy Crockett, one
of the few black men who could stand to live
in Glory River. Baron Gomes's skin
was notably darker than anybody

else's in his family, the Crocketts
and the Gomeses lived next door to each other,
and so the story of his conception,
a narrative of how it could have happened
between Baron's mother and Buddy Crockett—
maybe their paths crossed on a summer afternoon
when they were both out picking berries—
sprang to the mind of anybody from Glory
River who looked Baron in the face. The boy had
grown up hearing sly comments from grown-ups
and crude taunts from his schoolmates. So it was
an ongoing explosive situation
in the valley, because race isn't
an easy topic where feuds and killings
are common as Sunday dinner and insults
spark quarrels that last generations.
But these particular flames never caught
because Baron was a sweet child, and his mother
had died when he was in first grade. So he'd learned
to navigate in a world where he met
hostility and contempt along with
pity, sentiment, and plain old low-down,
gossipy curiosity.
                              Baron's problems
were school—which bored him—and his body—
which had grown faster than he could keep up with.
At twelve years old, Baron was six feet two
but comic-book skinny, so that he couldn't
walk to the store without tripping over his
size twelve shoes.
                              One morning the Mayor blocked
his way, and when Baron tried to step around
him, the Mayor was instantly back

in his way again. *Gotta get to school,*
damn dog, Baron said aloud, though he didn't
really care—but then he found himself—on a cool
frosty autumn morning—in this strange dance
with a demon dog. The boy must have thought
he was in a dream, because the animal bumped
him lightly or nudged him, then dodged or just
disappeared only to appear again behind Baron
or to the side, as if it meant to teach him
a certain way to move his body. Then somehow
Baron understood that he'd been challenged
to a race—he and the Mayor took off
toward the schoolhouse, and Baron later said
it felt like he was somewhere between flying
and floating. The Mayor barely beat him
to the door, into which Baron ducked, after
which he looked back out the window, but the dog
was nowhere to be seen. Baron's senses
were still elevated when classes began,
which made him pay attention in spite
of his old habits. And the Mayor was there
to meet him again when school was out—the two
of them raced again, out to the field beyond
Baron's house, where again the Mayor
took up the game of block and dodge that required
Baron to move his feet so quickly that he'd
have been mocked and humiliated if there'd
been anybody there to see the dance the dog
was teaching him.

             Within two weeks Baron Gomes
was Glory River Elementary's finest
athlete and best student, though a meanness
came up in him that he explained to me

in our interview. *Do you know what that dog*
did to me the last time I saw him? Bit me!
I don't mean he nipped me. He sank his teeth
in right here. Baron showed me the scars
on the thick muscle just below his thumb.
God damn thing bit me! And then just walked
on off and wouldn't have anything else
to do with me.
                        There were too many tales
of the Mayor's deeds for me to tell you
all of them. Shep Ogden never liked the dog,
claimed it hexed his cat so that it peed
on the furniture. Robbie Pickens said
the dog got him lost up on Dalton Mountain
and then disappeared. Jack Mabe confessed
that the dog sat beside him all one night
at the poker game down by the river, Jack won
more money than anybody ever had
in the long history of Glory River card
games, but then the next night the dog wasn't
there, and Jack lost all he'd won and then some.
Lila Schnell said the dog helped her get pregnant.
Deetum Dunford told about Elmer Clemons
offering a two hundred dollar reward
to anybody who'd shoot the Mayor,
but they had to bring Elmer the carcass
to prove they'd done it. All over the valley
men took out their shotguns, and a fair
number of them claimed to have shot the dog
point blank, only to find no carcass where
they'd seen him fall or else to see him get up
and scratch the dirt behind him like he'd
taken a leak and trot on off.

                This was
years ago that I did my fieldwork, wrote
my dissertation, the publication
of which led so many universities
to offer me jobs. More than once I've thought
that I owe my own good fortune to the Mayor
of Glory River. At first I thought this to be
the proper way of things—after all, I did
the work, I saw the symbolic possibility
in the dog, I shaped my writing shrewdly,
I followed the highest professional
standards.

                It is only now that I
approach retirement that I am besieged
with doubt—and why say doubt when it is
near certainty? Even if I saw it
with my own eyes, there was no such dog.
My interviewees lied to me. I was
grandly hornswoggled. Glory River had
its fun with me. And my university
doesn't want to hear that its Distinguished
Professor of Cultural Studies is
a consummate fool. Personally,
however, I'm old enough to understand
what a gift it was those years ago when
the people of Glory River took me in.
Which is to say that I welcome the black
dog that sometimes races through my dreams.

~ II ~
Mountain Spring

Ars Poetica

The poem, yes,
but also that goofy
random texture of the real . . .

As after volleyball something
stops my sneakered foot over a fallen leaf
that turns out to be a gorgeously

speckled green moth big as Tim Duncan's
left hand but fragile as damp tissue
and its wings all fluttery as if maybe

it's just hatched but its brief life
could flicker out
any second. Oh, I shall rescue

this elegant creature was my thought,
scooping it up,
transporting it to the Maple porch

and parking it on the arm
of a green chair—relieved not
to have its sticky little feet

prickling my palm, I was
dusting off my hands just when Arthur
came out the door, motoring toward somewhere

with his mind full of Shakespeare
and his complicated life back in Los Angeles
and his complex childhood back in Chicago

and all sixteen libraries worth
of concepts and information and memories and plans
archived up there in his brain

so that when I presented the moth to Arthur
—even though he and I go back to when
two years ago seated beside each other

on a plane to New Orleans, we discovered
we both worked for Bread Loaf—
I knew he didn't have time

for it, and the fact was
I didn't either, I had work to do upstairs
in my room, and besides, rescuing

a moth by transferring it
from grass under a tree to the arm of a chair
on the Maple porch was about as dumb an idea

as I've ever had, and I've had plenty—
so we both left the thing out there
in the dim light, fluttering

toward maybe another day of life or maybe
instant death, but either way it wasn't
there in the morning when I passed

by the chair on my way to breakfast, thinking
about my mother, which I do maybe
a hundred times in any single day,

not extended meditations, mind you,
just shots and flashes—
how she'd say a word,

a dress she wore,
something she liked to eat,
what she'd have thought about a green moth.

Sucker Punch

When I stepped out of the car, Boyce Patton
was waiting for me with his fist ready.
His weight in his swing, he caught me right on
the chin and broke my jaw because I'd said he

was a fuckface for calling me a son
of a bitch. To my mind, I got the best
of Boyce in the verbal competition,
and his winning the physical contest

was offset by the noble reputation
I got for having defended the good name
of my mother. Misinterpretation
lies in considering the bill that came

to our house from the orthodontist
who wired my jaws shut, so I had to let
my case rest. "Yes, our winner here may not
be clear," my dad said, "but we do know who lost."

Seer

Old horse-faced crazy Aunt Inez,
you who wore rags and spoke
only to Grandma Lawson after
you got out of the loony bin,

you who lived alone in that house
after Grandma Lawson died,
with Grandmama's hired man
delivering food, leaving it

for you out on the porch,
like you were a wild animal,
because you screamed at him
if he tried to come in, you,

my flesh and blood, who scared
the feeble wits out of many
an Ivanhoe boy peeking
through your window, because

you were God's personal malice-
faced, chalk-haired messenger
to the sane that craziness
could sink its teeth into anybody,

slather a person in saliva,
and spit him out a lunatic,
so that even the criminals
of Ivanhoe left you alone—you,

Aunt Inez, should know that Ida,
your sister, my grandmother,

once told me you made charts
of the stars for those you loved,

you drew maps that showed how
the Heavens were configured
at the hour of birth of someone
you thought worthy. Your sister spoke

in awe of those astrological
diagrams; those extraordinary
documents you made, a beauty
like which nobody had ever seen.

No End

A sonnet began the day I started
flirting with the band's youngest majorette
during marching practice—you'd think it'd
be forgotten by now, how the sweat

shone on her forehead, how the director
shouted and cursed as if preparing us
for battle and we were a bunch of soldiers
instead of backwoods kids—gawky, doofus

hillbillies good for homecoming parades
and halftime shows at football games. It came
to something—that flirtation—escapades
of learning to smoke, getting caught, that game

of whistle-stop in her basement. Dead five
years now. Almost unbearably alive.

Kindness

I've reached the age where I see a woman
two tennis courts away and recognize
her as Melva Stephens, whose bra she helped
me unfasten when she was fourteen
and I sixteen, and though of course I know
she died years ago, it's not strange Melva's
here in Burlington, where she never lived,
playing tennis, which she always hated.
David, she calls, *you were the only one
who ever truly appreciated my breasts!*

I don't walk over to talk to Melva,
because she would turn out to be someone
the sight of whom would make me feel ashamed
I'm no longer a boy a girl would want.
The blessing is—being around pretty
girls every day—I don't see so well, can't
hear half of what they say, and I'm losing
my sense of smell and taste. They're like ghosts,
these living beauties; whereas Melva—well,
she and I might go to the drive-in tonight.

Thirteen

In her worst moments of sadness
and outrage, my daughter Bess
ran into her closet, sat among
wads of clothes on the floor, and let

her muffled sobs reach me through two
shut doors. That year I walked home
for lunch one April day to witness
a couple kissing in the exact

middle of my street and thought, *What*
a charmingly romantic tableau
for a spring afternoon—I wish Bess
could see this—until it suddenly clicked

into my brain like the caption
to a photograph—*That is Bess!*
She's with goddamn sorry-assed
Sean Nunick, and they're supposed

to be in school this very moment!
Thirteen was a hard year for all of us,
and if I learned nothing else,
at least I came to understand

it was better for my Bess to be
out in the street in broad daylight
than to be buried deep down
in the dust of her dark closet.

Passenger

A body hits the carpeted concrete floor—
thud like a heavy thing dropped or thrown
makes me turn to see thin legs thrashing, white
sneakers, khaki slacks, four or five people
bent toward the figure and one kneeling
beside the fallen one.
                              I can't see her—
I've decided it's a woman, think she's
old, maybe dying here, now, three body
lengths from where I've sat down to read and pass
the time until my flight leaves.
                                        It must be
a daughter kneeling and calmly speaking
to the old woman. I can't hear the words,
but her tone seems to reach me—or maybe
I need to think someone is saying, *It's okay,
I'm here, you're not alone.*
                              I go back
to *Kafka on the Shore,* a perfect book
to read among ten thousand strangers, one
of them presently flying directly
to God, but my mind wants what it wants—*Gawk
at death!* it commands.
                              This time when I turn
the one who fell has risen—it's a girl,
maybe fifteen, and her mother, who'd knelt
beside her, now braces her with an arm
around her waist and brushes the girl's hair
away from her face.
                              Oh, what do I know?
I ask myself, and then answer, too, *Not
a God damn thing,* but that doesn't stop me

from marching forward with my thoughts—the child
must be an epileptic, the mother
must have witnessed seizures so many times . . .

                                                    Yes,
of course I talk to myself! Who doesn't?
There are as many of me as there were
milling strangers on D Concourse of O'Hare
Airport, each of us with plenty to say—
our ignorant, useless little prayers.

Two for the Reaper

1.

When spring finally arrives,
what we like to do just at dusk
on the first warm day is drive slowly
through that big Catholic graveyard
between Willard and Prospect,
Lindsey and Bess and Molly and I reading
from our rolled-down car windows
what we can make out from the gravestones,
our voices saying aloud the words,
our voices sounding out the names.

2.

As before you arrived,
the teenagers who became
your mother and father,
before they even met each other,
in the most private moments
of their separate lives
imagined you,

so may it be after you've gone,
your son smiling over
how you pronounced a word,
your granddaughter remembering
your secret, that you liked
to walk through the house naked
after your bath.

The Hardest Thing

In last night's dream a man had just begun
to murder me, and I'd started to struggle
like an animal in slaughter—like pigs
at my grandfather's farm screaming in the pen
as their throats were slit.
                                    It was my terror
that woke me,
                        and such a kindness to wake
into my ordinary life, my dear bed,
my house where my daughters have grown up,
the Vermont night outside my window,
with its little noises—raccoons and skunks
the worst I'd likely find out there in back,
clean clothes at my bedside, a warm shower
and a normal day my immediate
future.
                But the fear was still in me, still
crackling through my body like I'd been struck
by lightning and the current hadn't quite
stopped exploring my circuits. That bad dream
felt so real I knew I'd at least half lived
my death, maybe a dry run, a preview
of what's waiting for me.
                                    Emphysema
took my father, Alzheimer's my mother;
my brilliant brother became a half-wit;
I've jumped from planes, tasted dirt in Vietnam,
been close to divorce, fallen into disgrace,
feared for my daughters, flown into rages,
wept while I leaned against a downtown building,
and planned suicide,

                    but I can't even name
the hardest thing I've ever been through.
                                        Man
of ten thousand mistakes, writer, teacher,
loud talker, I hold only this useless
testimony: I who must have died go on
miraculously dreaming I'm alive.

Call Me Anonymous

The rain this morning made me feel old, made
me want to pull the covers over my head.
But in *A Man and a Woman*, it's that black
and white rain on the windshield that's stayed
with me forty years, not him, not her, not
anything they did. Loss is what rain brings
to mind—burying my grandmother, saying
goodbye to Linda, hospitals, funerals,
long grieving drives to someplace I'd rather
not go. Once I stripped naked on an old
tennis court in Vietnam. Many days of filth,
then a bath in the warm monsoon. Surely
I've kissed a girl in the rain, touched her face
and said, *God, you're something else.*
                                        I like how
in "Western Wind," this guy suddenly wants
to be back in bed with his sweetie. He's out
herding sheep, big cold rain blows in one day,
the storm splats him in the face, he grits
his teeth and says, *Where the hell are the* small
rains?! Jesus Christ, I wish I was back
in Ormskirk with Sheila, then because he's bored,
he changes a word here, a word there, makes it
into something to recite to the sheep
against the thunder and lightning. His first
night back in Chorley, he drinks too much ale
and hears himself bellowing to strangers
in the tavern. Someone says, *Hey, lad, what's*
that you just said? and the rest is the new
historicism. One thing leads to another—
first principle of everything living—
which is of course why I don't stay in bed
on rainy days. A young man knows the bad
news is that nothing lasts. An old man
knows the good news is that nothing lasts.

Double Crown

Two fingers in my mouth,
he braces the mold three
minutes against my teeth,
holds it steady, without

slack, tremor, or twitch.
The strength to do this
most people don't notice,
and Josh doesn't talk much

while he works. Seventy
years old now—fingers
and hands years younger—
his mind for dentistry

is sharper than it's
ever been, though he'd be
the first to admit nobody
cares about a dentist's

passion. It's a trance
he enters, especially
if the procedure's really
complicated and takes

time—like my broken-off
molar and its decayed
neighbor. The mold's stayed
in my mouth long enough,

and so Josh pries it out
and leaves me in the chair

to spit, rinse, touch where
my face feels just so odd.

Thugs attacked Josh upstairs
one Saturday a few years ago.
He was in the building alone
fixing the apartment up there

and because they saw his white
Mercedes out back, they went in
and demanded that he give them
money. When Josh tried to fight,

they nearly killed him, using
his own hammer on his face
and throat, ruining his voice
permanently. But his refusing

to die or even to retire
made me reconsider everything
I thought I knew about him.
When he speaks, there's a burr

in his voice that reminds me
what he went through, what
he survived. Imagining it
with my eyes closed while he

fashions the little sculpture
of new teeth in his workshop-
lab next door, I have to stop
because I can't stand my picture

of Josh lifting his educated
hands against the hammer.
I blink back to the chair.
Josh comes in—he's just created

a new part for my body—and sees
me staring at him, but of course
he has on his mask. "The worst
is over," he rasps. "Open please."

1970

That moment in *Hair*
where the whole cast
gets naked on stage?

Lindsey and I and Jean
and Ellsworth Bahrman
bought tickets, ate grass-

laced brownies, and rode
the Broadway Local downtown
to see the show, but we were way

back in the balcony,
I got sleepy, and Lindsey
had to give me an elbow

when it happened. Fact
is, I liked *Hair* best
the year before, at a party

in Roanoke, Virginia,
when somebody put on the record
(vinyl, of course), and a bunch

of Hollins girls started
to sing along—"I like black boys . . ."
and do a little footwork

that way you can step into it
when you're twenty years old,
about half-buzzed at a party

and somebody puts on a song
you like. But back to that night
when the lights came up,

and behold, there were the actors
wearing nothing but their bodies—
It was in the fall of 1970, audiences

were getting thinner every week,
and the way I see it now
is that I, David R. Huddle,

your basic twenty-eight-year-old,
moderately stoned, white,
liberal grad student, sat

right at the focal point at the exact
moment when the nation
made its final turn away from love

and generosity and toward greed,
hatred of the poor, bullying
the rest of the world, and pillaging

what's left of paradise. Please
forgive me, all of you lost
Americans. If—instead of nodding off

into a stupor—I'd just stayed
a little more alert and received
every megabyte of that vision, I might

have become the single human
being empowered to save
the planet from George W. Bush.

Tuba

The vibrating airstream
blown into its mouthpiece
contains spit, halitosis,
food particles, dust mites,
along with a few atoms of oxygen
that in 2435 BC circulated
among the pyramid-builders
of ancient Egypt. This stream
of air with assorted hitchhikers
serpentines through the metal
tube, navigating the valves
that process it into the exact
tone (an E-flat two octaves
below middle C) that was and is
its orchestral destiny—and now
this human-generated, machine-
shaped column of atmospheric
disturbance migrates toward
the larger and larger territory
of the horn's great shining bell,
out into the light of a summer
afternoon in the resort hotel's
concert garden—
           Ah the Note!
Finally the one note is sounded
at 3:13 p.m. on July 31, 1958,
behind the Martha Washington Inn
in Abingdon, Virginia. The spit,
the food, the dust mites, and even
the pyramids-educated oxygen
atoms—it all sweetly disperses
into the warm sunlight, a bass

E-flat worth suffering to hear,
the sonic equivalent of the grassy,
dandelioned lawn in Winslow Homer's
turn-of-the-century croquet game,
a tone so deep and sonorous it's God
harmonizing with the angels, a slice
of sound that lets me suddenly and only
for half an instant understand gazebos,
giraffes, the Jersey shore, China
far away in darkness, how
to unhook a brassiere as an act
of affection, the necessity of death,
and the life everlasting.

In the Boston Children's Hospital

Bess whom I'd thought might die—
for when she came out of surgery
she'd looked halfway to death—
was on the mend enough to be cranky
& demanding & it was maybe one
or two in the morning & I'd been
reading to her for so many pages
while she waked & slept & waked
& it was mostly dark in the room
just the circle of light by her bed
& I stopped & looked at her & saw
she was watching me & we were
quiet until she said very softly
"I'm sorry I've caused you so much
trouble" & I got so choked up
I sort of had to croak out what I had
to tell her which was that it had
been the great privilege of my life
to go through that awful experience
with her & I hadn't known that
until I said it & in me right then
were such sorrow & grief because both
her death & mine seemed to hover
by her bed & all around us & it felt
so much like pain I even winced & so
it was some minutes of sitting beside
my Bess who was getting better every
second that passed in that quiet room
with the nurses & orderlies passing
in the hallways before I leaned back
into the dark edge of her bedside
light & came to know the name of what
had so sharply pierced me was joy.

Water

1.

Valley farmland
beside a mountain:

A spring up there sent down
the coldest, sweetest water—

fifty years since my last sip,
my tongue still remembers

that black-dirt-dogwood
taste of the Blue Ridge.

2.

Between Bristol
and East Middlebury

springwater spouts
from a pipe beside the road—

I see people stopped there
filling plastic jugs.

I want what they want,
but I don't stop.

3.

A house, a car, antique furniture,
computers, phones, shelves of books,

stereos on every floor, a thousand CDs,
two TVs: I'm so rich if they were alive

my parents wouldn't know whether
to be proud of or embarrassed

by this life that feels to me
like nearly unbearable loss.

4.
At Costco now I buy cases of plastic
pints tightly sheathed in plastic, I

who once with my brothers, faces dusty
and guts scrambled by a washboard road,

tumbled from the back of our grandad's
red Dodge pickup and raced to the cow's

trough where the spigot stayed wide open,
and we thought the flow would never stop.